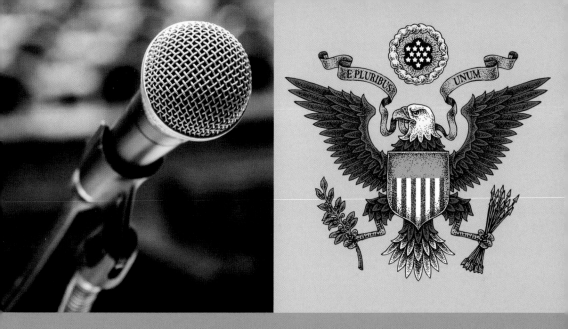

Understanding the

IMPEACHMENT PROCESS

WHAT'S UP

Alicia Klepeis

PowerKiDS press™

New York

Published in 2018 by **The Rosen Publishing Group, Inc.**
29 East 21st Street, New York, NY 10010

Cataloging-in-Publication Data
Names: Klepeis, Alicia.
Title: Understanding the impeachment process / Alicia Klepeis.
Description: New York : PowerKids Press, 2018. | Series: What's up with your government? |
    Includes index.
Identifiers: LCCN ISBN 9781538323267 (pbk.) | ISBN 9781538322307 (library bound) |
    ISBN 9781538323274 (6 pack)
Subjects: LCSH: Impeachments--United States--Juvenile literature. | Presidents--
    United States--Juvenile literature.
Classification: LCC KF4958.K55 2018 | DDC 342.73'062--dc23

First Edition

Developed and Produced by Focus Strategic Communications, Inc.
    Project Manager: Adrianna Edwards
    Editor: Ron Edwards
    Design and Composition: Ruth Dwight
    Copy editors: Adrianna Edwards, Francine Geraci
    Media Researchers: Adrianna Edwards, Paula Joiner
    Proofreader: Francine Geraci
    Index: Ron Edwards, Maddi Nixon

Photo Credits: Credit Abbreviations: LOC Library of Congress; NARA National Archives and
Records Administration; S Shutterstock; WC Wikimedia Commons. Position on the page: T:
top, B: Bottom, C: Center, L: left, R: right. Cover TL: TZIDO SUN/S, TR: Symonenko Viktoriia/S,
CL: Carsten Reisinger/S, B: Rob Crandall/S; 1 TL: TZIDO SUN/S, TR: Symonenko Viktoriia/S,
CL: Carsten Reisinger/S; 4: Ken Wolter/S; 5 L: Everett Historical/S, C: NARA/530679, R:
stocklight/S; 6: Everett Historical/S; 7: Frederic Legrand - COMEO/S; 8: Billion Photos/S;
9: Everett Historical/S; 10: Daderot/WC; 11: Everett Historical/S; 12: JPL Designs/S; 13:
Everett - Art/S; 14: Everett Historical/S; 15: C-SPAN; 16: Teguh Jati Prasetyo/S; 17 L: Everett
Collection/S, R: Featureflash Photo Agency/S; 18: Orhan Cam/S; 19: White House photo
by Susan Sterner; 20: C-SPAN; 22: sergign/S; 23: U.S. Department of Energy; 24: LOC/LC-
USZ61-985; 25: LOC/LC-USZ62-75616; 26: Frontpage/S; 27: Joseph Sohm/S; 28: New York
Public Library/1253444; Design Elements: Nella/S, tassita numsri/S.

Manufactured in the United States of America
CPSIA Compliance Information: Batch BW18PK: For Further Information contact
Rosen Publishing, New York, New York at 1-800-237-9932.

CONTENTS

IMPEACHMENT BASICS

IMPEACHMENT 101

The president is the highest-ranking member of the US government. They are the head of the executive branch, the branch of government responsible for putting into effect the laws passed by Congress. The president **appoints** the members of cabinet, as well as the heads of federal agencies. They are also in charge of the armed forces.

The US Presidential Seal is the official seal of the American president. It appears on the podium from which the president speaks to the public, on the sides of any vehicle carrying the president (such as Air Force One or the presidential limousine), and in the Oval Office.

FAST FACT

The original 13 colonies are represented in several places on the presidential seal: the eagle clutching 13 olives and leaves in its right claw, 13 arrows in its left claw, 13 red-and-white stripes on the shield, and 13 white clouds and stars above the eagle. Today, there are 50 stars around the eagle, representing the 50 states of the United States of America.

★ ★

PRESIDENTIAL ABUSE OF POWER

What happens if a US president abuses their power? What if they fail to uphold the responsibilities as president? In these situations, a president can be **impeached** and removed from office. What is impeachment? Read on to find out!

Impeached Presidents

Throughout American history, only three presidents have faced removal from office by impeachment. They were Andrew Johnson, Richard Nixon, and Bill Clinton. Johnson and Clinton were impeached but acquitted of any crime. Nixon was about to be impeached but resigned.

Andrew Johnson was impeached in 1868.

Richard Nixon resigned in 1974 before being impeached.

Bill Clinton was impeached in 1998.

WHAT IS IMPEACHMENT?

Impeachment is a power held by Congress—the legislative branch of government that consists of the House of Representatives and the Senate.

The word "impeach" means to formally charge a public official with misconduct in office. Sometimes people also use the word to mean the removal from office of a public official.

The impeachment process is designed to punish officers of the executive branch and the judicial branch (the branch relating to judges and the courts) who abuse their power.

Congressman Thaddeus Stevens addresses the House of Representatives on March 2, 1868. His was the last speech on the impeachment of President Andrew Johnson.

Impeachment Around the Globe

The United States is not the only country to use impeachment as a way to get rid of officials who have acted improperly while in office. In 2016, both South Korea and Brazil impeached their presidents. Brazil removed its president, Dilma Rousseff, from office. Rousseff's vice president replaced her. In March 2017, South Korean President Park Geun-hye was also removed from office. By law, the country had to elect a new president within 60 days.

Dilma Rousseff

Park Geun-hye

FAST FACT

If a US president is impeached and found guilty, the vice president takes over the presidency. The legislatures of every US state, except for Oregon, also can impeach executive or judicial officials at the state level.

★ ★

7

WHO CAN BE IMPEACHED?

The impeachment process is lengthy and complex. Article 2, section 4 of the US Constitution says:

*"The President, Vice President and all Civil Officers of the United States, shall be removed from Office on Impeachment for, and conviction of, **Treason**, **Bribery**, or other High Crimes and Misdemeanors."*

Civil officers of the United States include federal judges, cabinet officials, and Supreme Court justices—all of whom can be impeached.

The impeachment process does not apply to all federal officials. According to today's rules and laws, members of Congress cannot be impeached.

The US Constitution lists many possible reasons for impeachment.

William Blount, America's First Impeached Official

William Blount was one of the first senators from Tennessee. He was also one of the signers of the Constitution. President John Adams told Congress that his administration had uncovered a conspiracy involving Blount. The House of Representatives voted to impeach Blount in July 1797. The Senate ordered Blount to answer impeachment charges before a committee. Blount didn't show up. In February 1798, the Senate prepared for his trial, although Congress was still not certain whether senators could be impeached. In fact, the Senate dismissed the charges a year later because it decided that impeaching senators was not within their power.

William Blount was accused of plotting with the British.

FAST FACT

Today, members of the House of Representatives and the Senate can be removed from office only by a two-thirds vote by their respective chambers.

★ ★

HISTORY OF IMPEACHMENT IN AMERICA

WHY WE HAVE AN IMPEACHMENT PROCESS

Why does the United States have an impeachment process? The answer goes all the way back to our nation's Founding Fathers. In 1787, delegates from all states except Rhode Island met in Philadelphia. These delegates worked to strengthen the United States' national government by writing the Constitution.

The Framers of the Constitution wanted to be sure that our country had a means by which government officials who were believed to be guilty of serious misconduct could be tried and removed from office if they were found guilty.

THE FOUNDING FATHERS AT WORK

The Founding Fathers wanted to have a way to get rid of government officials who had committed crimes or abused their privileges of office. However, they didn't want the procedure to be too simple. If the impeachment process were easy, it might be used too often. It might also be used for purely political reasons. For example, if an official wanted a political rival to be kicked out of office, he might suggest impeachment. That wouldn't be fair.

Founding Father George Mason suggested that "maladministration" could be a reason to impeach someone. Mason's term meant running the government poorly. But James Madison and Gouverneur Morris said that term wasn't clear enough. They worried it would allow the Senate to affect officials' term in office too easily.

George Mason attended the Philadelphia Constitutional Convention and helped draft parts of the US Constitution.

FAST FACT

Britain has used the impeachment process since the fourteenth century but has rarely used it since the early nineteenth century. The US model of impeachment is strongly based on this British legal tradition.

★ ★

CHECKS AND BALANCES

Another reason that the Framers wanted to have an impeachment process has to do with the system of checks and balances provided by the Constitution.

The Founding Fathers wanted the three branches of government—executive, legislative, and judicial—to be independent of one another. They gave each branch ways to keep the power of the other branches in check. For example, even though Congress (the legislative branch) makes the nation's laws, the president (the executive branch) can **veto** proposed laws.

THE THREE BRANCHES OF GOVERNMENT

LEGISLATIVE
(makes laws)

EXECUTIVE
(carries out laws)

JUDICIAL
(evaluates laws)

PURPOSE OF IMPEACHMENT

Impeachment is a way for the legislative branch to keep the judicial and executive branches' power in check. For example, Supreme Court justices are appointed for life. What might happen if one were abusing their power? Without the impeachment process, that abuse could go on for a very long time.

James Madison (1751–1836) argued in favor of impeachment.

Are Elections Enough of a Check?

Some Founding Fathers argued against impeachment of executive officials. They felt elections every four years would keep the president's power in check. But James Madison disagreed. He argued that elections weren't enough of a check if a president were abusing the power of office, or if a president were too ill or disabled to fulfill the responsibilities.

WHAT OFFENSES ARE WORTHY OF IMPEACHMENT?

The US Constitution outlines the offenses that can lead to impeachment. Article 2, section 4 states that public officials can be impeached for "Treason, Bribery, or other High Crimes and Misdemeanors."

Treason is the crime of betraying one's country, such as trying to overthrow the government or plotting to kill the nation's leader. Bribery is the act of giving or promising something to a person in order to influence a decision or action dishonestly or illegally. An example would be a defendant paying a federal judge $10,000 for a verdict of "not guilty."

Aaron Burr

Aaron Burr was the third vice president of the United States (1801–1805). He was accused of treason in 1807 after plotting the invasion of Mexico. He was tried for treason, but was acquitted.

Aaron Burr's political career ended after he killed Alexander Hamilton in a duel in 1804.

HIGH CRIMES AND MISDEMEANORS

"High crimes and misdemeanors" are crimes that public officials commit against their government. Let's look at some examples.

Congress has impeached federal judges for many reasons. One is showing favoritism on the bench. Another is for filing false income tax returns. Lying under oath, and even being drunk on a regular basis, can also fall under this category.

Thomas Porteous

Only 15 federal judges have ever been impeached, and only eight have been convicted and removed from the bench. Most recently, in 2010, Judge Thomas Porteous of Louisiana was impeached. He was tried in the US Senate, convicted, and removed from

JUDGE THOMAS PORTEOUS IMPEACHMENT TRIAL
Senate Impeachment Trial Committee
Hart Senate Office Building

Judge Thomas Porteous attends his Senate impeachment trial.

HOW THE IMPEACHMENT PROCESS WORKS

CHARGES ARE MADE

Impeachment is a complicated process. The US Constitution gives the House of Representatives the sole power of bringing charges against the president, vice president, and all US civil officers.

How does the impeachment process start? A House of Representatives member can declare a charge of impeachment. Nonmembers of the House can suggest that the House consider impeachment of a federal judge. An example of a nonmember could be the Judicial Conference of the United States, a national association of senior judges. The president can also send a message to the House to consider impeachment of a particular official.

There are several ways for the impeachment process to start.

Bill Clinton

Monica Lewinsky

Bill Clinton Impeachment

Kenneth Starr was appointed a Federal Court of Appeals judge by President Ronald Reagan in 1983. President George H.W. Bush appointed him solicitor general in 1989. In 1994, Starr was appointed to the Ethics in Government Committee. As the head of that committee, he investigated President Bill Clinton and his wife Hillary for possible financial corruption. As an independent counsel, Starr brought Bill Clinton's impeachable offenses to the attention of the House. A 1997 Starr report stated that Clinton had lied under oath about his relationship with Monica Lewinsky, a White House intern at the time. This led to Clinton's impeachment in 1998.

FAST FACT

After President Clinton was impeached, he was acquitted by the Senate in 1999.

★ ★ ★ ★ ★ ★ ★ ★ ★ ★ ★ ★ ★ ★ ★ ★ ★ ★ ★

RESOLUTION AND HOUSE VOTE

Impeachment charges come to the House of Representatives. Then the House Judiciary Committee considers evidence to see whether the charges are serious enough to hold impeachment hearings. This committee must have a two-thirds **majority** vote to continue. Otherwise, the impeachment process ends.

House Judiciary Committee

The House Judiciary Committee is one of 20 standing (permanent) committees of the House of Representatives. These groups consist of six to 50 members who meet regularly to discuss issues such as legislation or budgets.

The House of Representatives meets in the Capitol building in Washington, DC.

FAST FACT

The House of Representatives can overturn a Judiciary Committee vote if the House majority votes against impeachment.

★ ★

HOUSE OF REPRESENTATIVES

What happens if the House Judiciary Committee decides that the charges are serious enough to hold hearings? It will draft a **resolution**. This statement officially impeaches the individual in question. The resolution will list the specific charges of misconduct. These charges are called articles of impeachment. The resolution will be reported to the full House of Representatives.

The whole House of Representatives hears all of the charges. Then they debate the articles of impeachment. When the debate ends, the House holds a vote.

Representatives vote separately on each article of impeachment. There must be a majority vote in the House. Otherwise, the case will not proceed before the Senate.

SENATE TRIAL AND VOTE

Members of the Senate hear the articles of impeachment.
But the House of Representatives still has another job.
The House appoints managers to lead the impeachment
trial. This trial takes place in the Senate.

Impeachment Managers

Representative Adam Schiff was the chief Democratic
impeachment manager at the impeachment trial of
Judge Thomas Porteous in 2010. Schiff is a Democratic
congressman for the California district that
includes Hollywood.

Adam Schiff leads
the impeachment
trial of Judge
Thomas Porteous.

LIVE
5:15 am PT

JUDGE THOMAS PORTEOUS IMPEACHMENT TRIAL
REP. ADAM SCHIFF
D-California, 29th District
Chief Democratic Impeachment Manager

THE SENATE

The Senate acts as judge and jury in most impeachment trials, unless it is the president who is being impeached. In this case, the chief justice of the Supreme Court presides over the trial in the Senate.

An impeachment trial is much like other trials. The accused answers questions, and so do other witnesses. The questions focus on the acts considered worthy of impeachment.

Senators vote on each article of impeachment separately. To find someone found guilty of any article, there must be a two-thirds vote among those senators who are present.

The Senate isn't required to vote on all of the impeachment articles brought before it. If an individual has already been found guilty on one or more impeachment articles, then the Senate may choose not to vote on the remaining articles.

FAST FACT

During an impeachment trial, Senate rules require that everyone be silent—otherwise, they could go to jail!

★ ★ ★ ★ ★ ★ ★ ★ ★ ★ ★ ★ ★ ★ ★ ★ ★ ★ ★ ★

EARLY IMPEACHMENT CASES

PUNISHMENTS FOR IMPEACHMENT

What happens to an official who has been impeached? How are they punished?

A simple majority vote disqualifies an impeached person from holding office in the future.

If any article of impeachment gets the necessary two-thirds vote in the Senate, the convicted person is immediately removed from office. But there's another possible punishment. The Senate can also disqualify the person from ever holding political office again.

FAST FACT

In Great Britain, the death penalty was among the punishments allowed for an impeachment. The last British official to be impeached was Henry Dundas, First Viscount Melville, in 1806. However, he was acquitted.

★ ★ ★ ★ ★ ★ ★ ★ ★ ★ ★ ★ ★ ★ ★ ★ ★ ★ ★

ADDITIONAL PUNISHMENTS

There may be additional punishments for an impeached person, depending on the reasons for impeachment. The Senate cannot impose criminal penalties on people. Who can decide on punishments for crimes committed while in office? The court system can impose additional fines and jail time, if necessary.

In January 2017, Rod Blagojevich filed to have his sentence commuted, or shortened. However, President Obama chose not to shorten his 14-year sentence.

Rod Blagojevich

In December 2008, Illinois Governor Rod Blagojevich was arrested and charged with corruption. The Illinois House and Senate voted 114 to 1 to impeach the governor. He was convicted and removed from office. In April 2009, a federal grand jury indicted Blagojevich on charges of bribery and corruption. In June 2011, Blagojevich was convicted of 17 of 20 charges. In December 2011, he was sentenced to 14 years in federal prison.

PEACHMENT OF PRESIDENT
DREW JOHNSON

An unusual event occurred in February 1868. For the first time in American history, the House of Representatives impeached a sitting president—Andrew Johnson. In 1867, Congress had passed the Tenure of Office Act. This law prevented the president from dismissing appointed government officials without the Senate's permission.

Edwin Stanton

A central figure in the impeachment of Andrew Johnson was Edwin M. Stanton. The Ohio lawyer had been chosen as the 27th US secretary of war by Abraham Lincoln on January 20, 1862. After Lincoln's assassination in 1865, Andrew Johnson, who was Lincoln's vice president, became president. It was not long before Johnson clashed with Stanton over policies toward the conquered Confederate States. Johnson felt that Stanton was too hard and unforgiving toward the South. He suspended Stanton as secretary of war on August 12, 1867. The Senate almost immediately voted to reinstate Stanton. When Johnson vowed to dismiss Stanton again, Congress voted to impeach Johnson for violating the Tenure of

Edwin M. Stanton

IMPEACHMENT TRIAL

A few days later, the House of Representatives impeached President Johnson. The House voted 126 to 47 in favor of impeachment. Besides violating the Tenure of Office Act, Johnson was also accused of disgracing and ridiculing the Congress of the United States through several speeches.

President Johnson had a trial in the Senate. It started on March 4 and lasted 11 weeks. In May 1868, Johnson escaped being removed from office by only one vote short of the two-thirds majority required to convict him.

Congressman Thaddeus Stevens addresses the House of Representatives on March 2, 1868, at the impeachment trial of Andrew Johnson.

FAST FACT

The Tenure of Office Act was declared unconstitutional in 1926.

★ ★ ★ ★ ★ ★ ★ ★ ★ ★ ★ ★ ★ ★

TWENTIETH-CENTURY IMPEACHMENTS

Congress impeached two US presidents in the twentieth century: Richard Nixon and Bill Clinton.

RICHARD NIXON

In August 1974, the House Judiciary Committee voted on articles of impeachment against President Nixon. What did Nixon do? He was involved in what became known as the Watergate scandal, after his colleagues stole information from the Democratic National Committee headquarters in the Watergate office building in Washington, DC.

One charge against Nixon was misuse of presidential power. Another was **obstruction** of justice. He resigned before impeachment proceedings could begin.

The Watergate complex, which contains offices, apartments, and a hotel, was built in Washington, DC, in 1967. Five years later, it would house the headquarters of the Democratic National Committee.

FAST FACT

Richard Nixon remains the only US president ever to resign from office.

★ ★ ★ ★ ★ ★ ★ ★ ★ ★ ★ ★ ★

BILL CLINTON

The House of Representatives voted to impeach President Clinton in December 1998. The charges against him were perjury and obstruction of justice. Both charges were related to an investigation of his relationship with a White House intern, Monica Lewinsky.

President Clinton went through the full impeachment process, including a trial in the Senate. The two charges against him each required a separate vote. Neither one managed to receive the two-thirds vote needed to impeach him. So the Senate declared Clinton not guilty on both charges.

During the voting for President Bill Clinton's impeachment, 50 senators voted not guilty to the charge of obstruction, and 50 voted guilty. On the charge of perjury, 55 senators voted not guilty, while the other 45 voted guilty.

THE IMPEACHMENT PROCESS: STILL USEFUL TODAY?

The impeachment process has been around since the earliest days of the United States. The Founding Fathers chose impeachment as one way to maintain the checks and balances system of government.

Some people say that the impeachment process is too lengthy. Supporters would point out, however, that it works. It ensures that politicians are not impeached for the wrong reasons. Presidents, vice presidents, cabinet members, and federal judges who abuse their power of office can be impeached.

Samuel Chase

On January 5, 1804, the House of Representatives began investigating Supreme Court Justice Samuel Chase on charges of political bias. His lengthy impeachment trial lasted for over a year. However, on March 1, 1805, the Senate voted to acquit him.

Chase remains the only US Supreme Court justice ever to have been impeached.

Impeachments Throughout US History

Since its first session in 1789, the House of Representatives has begun impeachment proceedings over 60 times. However, fewer than a third of these proceedings have resulted in full impeachments. Officials who have been impeached include 15 federal judges, two presidents, one cabinet secretary, and one senator. In that same time, the Senate has convicted and removed only eight people from office—all of them federal judges.

IMPEACHED US JUDGES

DATE OF TRIAL	NAME OF JUDGE	COURT OR DISTRICT	RESULTS
1803	John Pickering	New Hampshire	Convicted
1804	Samuel Chase	Supreme Court	Acquitted
1830	James Hawkins Peck	Missouri	Acquitted
1862	West Hughes Humphreys	Tennessee	Convicted
1873	Mark Delahay	Kansas	Resigned
1904	Charles Swayne	Florida	Acquitted
1912	Robert Wodrow Archibald	Commerce Court	Convicted
1926	George Washington English	Illinois	Resigned
1933	Harold Louderback	California	Acquitted
1936	Halstead Lockwood Ritter	Florida	Convicted
1986	Harry Claiborne	Nevada	Convicted
1988	Alcee Hastings	Florida	Convicted
1989	Walter Nixon	Mississippi	Convicted
2009	Samuel Kent	Texas	Resigned
2010	Thomas Porteous	Louisiana	Convicted

GLOSSARY

acquit — to declare innocent of a crime or wrongdoing

appoint — to choose for some job or office

bribery — the offense of offering payment or granting a favor in an attempt to influence a decision or action

conspiracy — a secret plan by a person or group to do something harmful or unlawful

corruption — dishonest behavior by someone in power, typically involving bribery

counsel — a lawyer (or group of lawyers) who is conducting a case

impeach — to charge the holder of a public office, such as the president, with misconduct

indict — to formally accuse and charge with a serious crime

majority — a percentage or number greater than half of the total

obstruction — the deliberate blocking of a legal process

perjury — the offense of lying while under oath, as in a court

resolution — a formal statement of the wishes, feelings, or decision of a group

treason — betrayal of one's country, such as by attempting to overthrow the government or by trying to kill the head of state

veto — the power of a head of government to prevent a bill passed by a legislature from becoming law

FURTHER INFORMATION

BOOKS

Archer, Jules. *Watergate: A Story of Richard Nixon and the Shocking 1972 Scandal*. New York: Sky Pony Press, 2015.

Sonneborn, Liz. *The United States Constitution*. Heinemann, 2012.

ONLINE

PowerKids Press has developed an online list of websites related to the subject of this book. This site is updated regularly. Please use this link to access the list:

www.powerkidslinks.com/wuwyg/impeachment

INDEX